Vae's REAL Life FAIRYTALE

Written By: Veronica Hood
Inspired by Vae Evans

I dedicate this book to my Daughter Vae Evans. Vae, I want you to always remember your "why" in life. Never let anything hold you back. You can do anything you put your mind to, and always remember that you are enough!

My Inspiration
My "WHY"
My number one reason why I cannot give up!

-Vae Evans

I Challenge

Name: _____

to always follow your dreams in life.

Hi,

I'm Vae, and I am a real-life beauty.
I am little in size but a major cutie.

Starting my first business (Vae's Lemonade) at just one month old, of course Mommy and Daddy helps and we always sell it fresh and cold.

Learning to swim at six months old, seems like a dream. I'm doing it in real life and one day maybe I will be on an amazing swim team.

I love to learn with Mommy and Daddy we watch many shows like "Vocabularry". They teach me songs, my ABC'S, always tell me I'm beautiful and read to me.

Going to the park with Daddy is always fun. We feed the ducks and enjoy the sun.

My mom and I do affirmations every day she says "come on, pretty lady, look in the mirror and say "I am beautiful, I am smart, I deserve the world, I can be anything I want to be, and no one or nothing can stop me!"

I am just getting started and have much more to do. Always remember let nothing get in the way of making your dreams come true.

The beginning, NOT the end!

Vae's Challenge

I challenge you to think of some affirmations for yourself, write them down, and say them to yourself in a mirror every day.

_____ Affirmations

1. _____

2. _____

3. _____

4. _____

5. _____

6. _____

7. _____

8. _____

9. _____

10. _____

Vae's Challenge
It's time for a fun project!

With the help of an adult you are going to create a Vision Board (A tool used to help clarify, concentrate, and maintain focus on a specific life goal. A board on which you place images and words that represent whatever you want to be, do, or have in your life).

1. Write down all of your life goals.

    _____

    _____

    _____

    _____

    _____

2. Find pictures and words that describe your goals
    For example you can cut pictures and words out of an old magazine.

3. Create your vision board.

4. Look at your vision board daily so that you can work towards your goals in life.

Vae's Big thank you

I would like to take this time to thank each and every person that has or will ever support me in my life. Also, I would like to thank each child on earth because we are the future. Lastly, I would like to thank my Mom and Dad because without them there would be no me.

Always remember you are never too young to follow your dreams!!!

Connect with Vae

Post your work on social media tag Us on

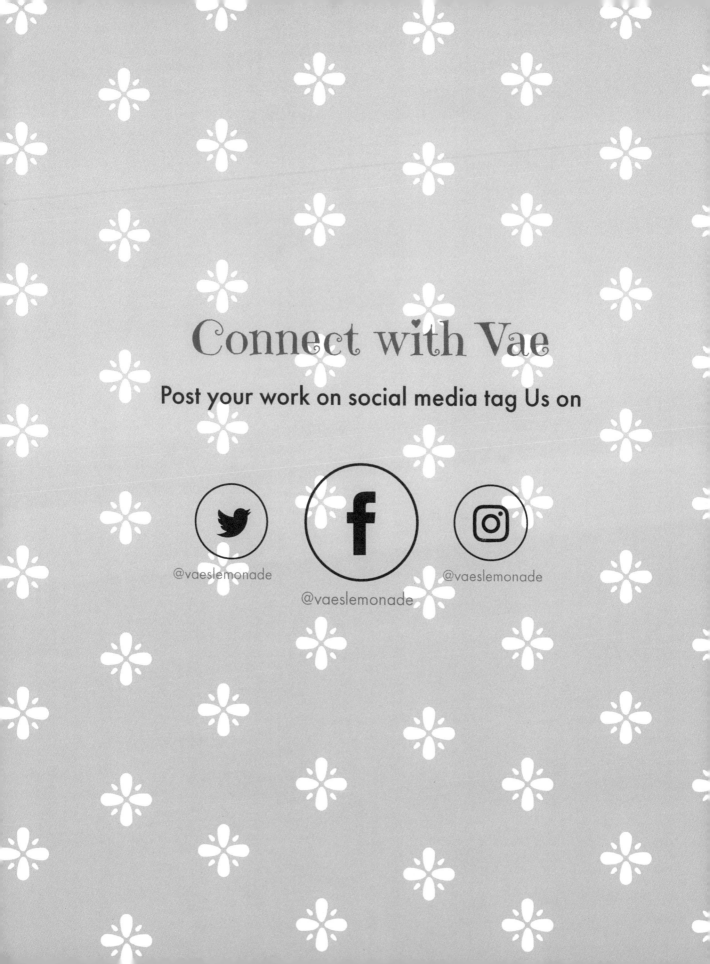

@vaeslemonade

@vaeslemonade

@vaeslemonade

About the Author

Veronica Hood born and raised in Atlanta, Ga. She is the proud mother of Vae Evans. She is the founder of the I'm MAD Project (Making A Difference) and strongly believes in giving back to the younger generation as they are the future. She spends most of her days making a difference in the lives of others while running her daughter's Business (Vae's Lemonade). She is a motivational speaker that firmly believes in the power of affirmations. In closing she encourages everyone to follow their dreams, stay true to themselves, and let nothing hold them back from accomplishing their dreams in life!

Made in the USA
Columbia, SC
25 February 2021